An Introduction to Coping with

Depression

2nd Edition

Lee Brosan
and
Brenda Hogan

ROBINSON

ROBINSON

First published in Great Britain in 2007 by Constable & Robinson Ltd

This revised and updated edition published in 2018 by Robinson

Copyright © Lee Brosan and Brenda Hogan, 2007, 2018

1 3 5 7 9 10 8 6 4 2

The moral rights of the authors have been asserted.

A CIP catalogue record for this book
is available from the British Library.

Important note
This book is not intended as a substitute for medical advice
or treatment. Any person with a condition requiring medical
attention should consult a qualified medical practitioner
or suitable therapist.

ISBN: 978-1-47214-021-0

Typeset in Bembo by Initial Typesetting Services, Edinburgh
Printed and bound in Great Britain by CPI Group (UK) Ltd,
Croydon CR0 4YY.

Papers used by Robinson are from well-managed forests
and other responsible sources.

Robinson
An imprint of
Little, Brown Book Group
Carmelite House
50 Victoria Embankment
London EC4Y 0DZ

An Hachette UK Company
www.hachette.co.uk
www.littlebrown.co.uk

Contents

About This Book

Most of us feel low at certain times in our lives, but find that the feeling improves after a short while. Unfortunately, sometimes these ordinary every-day lows do not lift and depression may start to take over.

This booklet will help you overcome depression. Part 1 describes the symptoms of depression and explains the way in which these are kept going. Part 2 looks at practical skills you can use to combat the symptoms of depression.

Many people find it most helpful to read and work through the booklet from start to finish, and to go back and review what they've read. But you may prefer just to dip into the parts that seem most relevant to you. It's often helpful to write things down, and Part 2 of the book contains several exercises, with worked examples to guide you. It would probably be helpful to read chapter seven on negative thinking and depression, since those ideas underlie a lot of what we have found to be helpful in overcoming depression.

When you're feeling depressed it can be difficult to believe that it can ever get better. But depression can improve, and you can learn to do something about it. You may not see the results immediately, but if you continue to work at it, then the chances are high that you'll start to see changes. There may be times when you feel that things are improving and then they get worse. Don't despair. The course of recovery is never smooth and setbacks are common. Keep going!

This booklet is designed for you to use on your own. However, if you find that you don't make as much progress as you wish, or if it all feels too much to try on your own, then go to your GP and talk about alternatives. Medication, or help from a qualified therapist, may be helpful for you. It can also be helpful to show the booklet to a trusted friend or family member who could help you to go through it – and who might also find it helpful to better understand what you are going through.

Good luck!

Lee Brosan and Brenda Hogan

Part 1: ABOUT DEPRESSION

1

What is Depression?

Depression is a very painful and sadly very common human experience. It affects about one in five people at some point in their lives. For some people, it might happen only once and pass quite quickly of its own accord. For others, depression may last longer or come back several times and require treatment. Since many people try to hide their depression, you may not have realised how common it is.

Symptoms of depression

Some of the most common symptoms of depression are listed below.

- **Depressed mood**. Feeling low, sad, miserable, hopeless or irritable. Sometimes people feel bleak, numb and empty.

- **Losing interest and enjoyment in activities you previously enjoyed**. Nothing seems fun anymore. Things that used to be enjoyable feel like a chore. Motivation to do almost anything is very low.

- **Self-criticism and guilt**. Feeling that you are bad, useless, inadequate and worthless.

- **Pessimism**. Expecting that things will go badly rather than well. Thoughts such as 'This won't work out right' are common.

- **Hopelessness**. Losing all hope that things can get better and feeling that the future holds nothing but more problems and more depression. Thoughts like 'There's no point in trying'.

- **Loss of energy**. Feeling tired all the time.

- **Reduced activity**. Sometimes this gets to the point where people do very little, especially when compared to their life before depression.

- **Withdrawal from social activities**. It's common for people to stop returning phone calls and to avoid occasions that involve socialising with other people.

- **Difficulty concentrating**. You may find it harder to read a book or watch a TV programme.

- **Memory difficulties**. Problems with short-term memory are common; for example, forgetting your keys when you go out. There are other memory changes as well: for example, it's easier to remember bad things than good things that have happened.

- **Changes in sleep patterns**. You may have a lot of difficulty sleeping or feel as though you could sleep endlessly.

- **Changes in appetite and weight**. Loss of appetite or 'comfort eating' often result in unwelcome changes in weight.

- **Loss of interest in sex**.

- **Thoughts of death**. These range from thoughts that it wouldn't be so bad to be killed accidentally to actively making plans for suicide. *If you are having frequent or serious thoughts about suicide then you need to get professional help as soon as possible. If you are already seeing a mental health professional, contact them right away to talk about your thoughts. If not, make an appointment with your GP right away so that you can talk about these thoughts and how you can get help. If you are having very frequent thoughts about suicide and are unable to see your GP straight away, try contacting the Samaritans (see back of book for contact details).*

The symptoms of depression can be roughly classified into four main groups:

- **Mood symptoms**, often considered to be the core symptoms of depression.

- **Physical symptoms**, such as changes in sleep patterns, appetite, weight and energy.

- **Cognitive ('thinking') symptoms**, including difficulties in concentrating, making decisions or working out problems, as well as memory difficulties. You may also start to think very negatively.

- **Behavioural symptoms**, such as withdrawal from social and other activities you previously enjoyed.

2

Myths about Depression

You may have particular beliefs about depression that are not necessarily true and sometimes these beliefs can make depression even worse. It's important to look at these misconceptions and to try to get to a more realistic way of seeing things. We have called these beliefs 'myths'.

Myth no. 1: *Nothing bad has happened to me. There's no reason why I should be depressed. It must be my fault.*

Reality: Sometimes it's very hard to understand why you have become depressed, and you end up thinking that the depression is in some way your fault. But in almost every case, with some help, you can see what has gone on in a different way – in a way that means that you don't have to blame yourself for feeling like that.

Myth no. 2: *I don't know why people say this is depression. I've always felt like this.*

Reality: This is common if you've felt unhappy all your life. It's very difficult to see the way you feel is depression, not just how you are. It can be even more difficult to believe that it will change if you've always felt like this – but it can.

Myth no. 3: *Depression is biological – like a switch going in your brain – and there is nothing you can do about it. Only pills can make the difference.*

Reality: It is true that medication can help. Research has shown that both medication and the strategies described in this book (focused on making helpful changes to the way you think and behave) are helpful in overcoming depression. Even if you are taking medication, you may be able to speed up your recovery by trying to make changes in the way you think and behave. Making these kinds of positive changes can help you recover from a current episode of depression, and they can also help prevent future problems with mood – even after you have stopped taking medication. It might be helpful to remember that even medical conditions that are entirely biological can be helped by making lifestyle changes – for example, diabetes can be treated with medication but can also be effectively managed by making behavioural changes, or a combination of both.

Myth no. 4: *Other people can cope with their lives without getting depressed – much worse things happen to them. I'm just weak and pathetic – I should be able to cope.*

Reality: It can look as if everyone else is getting on with life and coping better than you. This is partly because you tend to focus only on people who are coping and not notice those who aren't. It may also be because people go to great lengths to hide their true feelings when they are having trouble coping, so you might not notice that they are finding things difficult. It's important to remember that the feeling that you can't cope is a symptom of depression, and isn't a sign that you are weak and pathetic.

Myth no. 5: *I should just be able to pull my socks up and get on with things. I shouldn't need help from anyone else. Anyway, talking about yourself is just selfish and self-indulgent and doesn't help.*

Reality: If it were this simple, no one would ever be depressed. But you can't just 'snap out of it' and talking about yourself in a constructive way has been shown to be very helpful.

Myth no. 6: *Why should I take medication? It won't help. It can't change the things that are making me depressed.*

Reality: It's true that medication won't change the things in your life that are troublesome. But it can help to make you feel better and therefore help you to cope with your problems in a different way. Taking medication can help 'turn down the volume' on your symptoms, making it easier to make helpful changes in the way you think and behave. Together, this can be a very effective way to recover from depression.

What Causes Depression?

People become depressed for a wide variety of reasons. The main, important factors are listed below.

Genetics

You may inherit genes that make you more likely to develop depression. If people in your family have suffered from depression, you may be at risk. However, a family may have a high rate of depression because of the way people in the family behave towards each other, rather than because of the direct effect of genes.

Brains and biology

When you are depressed, changes occur in the brain, both in levels of special brain chemicals and in electrical activity. These changes tend to be especially marked if you suffer a lot of physical symptoms of depression: difficulty sleeping, change

in appetite and lethargy. However, when you recover from depression, these changes are reversed
and brain activity goes back to normal. It's difficult
to say whether these changes cause depression, but
they certainly accompany it.

Other physical aspects may also contribute to depression. For example, poor sleep can lead to fatigue,
irritability and difficulty in problem-solving, which
can set the stage for depression to develop. Or being
'run down' may make it more likely that you will
get depressed.

Difficult life experiences

Early experience

You may have had a difficult life from an early age
caused by practical difficulties, abuse or neglect.
Your parents may have separated or died or you
may have had a tough time at school; perhaps you
were bullied. In these cases, you're more vulnerable
to developing depression, particularly if your early
experiences taught you to think negatively.

Life events

Things might have been going reasonably well for
you until something awful happened: marriage

break-up, losing a job or the death of a loved one. It's very common to get depressed when you face a very stressful life event.

Ongoing stress

Sometimes depression is brought on by problems that seem to go and on without any solution in sight. Perhaps you have financial or relationship problems or suffer from a chronic illness. Ongoing stress can lead to negative thinking, which increases the risk of depression. Often a combination of these factors is responsible for depression. The importance of each factor varies from person to person.

Why is It So Hard to Stop Feeling Depressed?

Once you are depressed, you experience many changes that can actually keep depression going.

Behaviour

Depression usually changes the way you behave. You may withdraw from family and friends, stop making and returning phone calls or visit friends and family less often. This can make you feel isolated and lonely, which makes you feel worse. You may miss the comfort of company, but may think that other people have no interest in you or can't or shouldn't be bothered.

Depression often stops you doing things you used to enjoy, such as reading, sports, going for walks, hobbies or playing with children. Often you feel too tired or unmotivated to do these things, and the less you do, the less you feel able to do; often you simply stop enjoying them, which can be very discouraging.

It's also common when you're depressed to neglect your appearance. You may stop dressing smartly and buying new clothes or stop shaving or wearing make-up. In extreme cases, you may wash or bathe less often and wear the same clothes day after day. It's not unusual to stop exercising. Unfortunately, poor self-care and less exercise can deepen depression by making you feel worse about yourself and generally discouraged.

The small but necessary day-to-day tasks, such as running errands, opening the post, paying bills and cleaning the house, may also slide. When you struggle with depression you may find yourself putting off these jobs or neglecting them altogether. As your 'To-Do' list grows, you may feel overwhelmed, inadequate and unable to cope.

Together, these changes in behaviour can make it seem as if life has nothing good to offer and is just a series of insurmountable hurdles. A lack of rewarding activity seems to be very important in keeping depression going.

Thoughts

When you're depressed, you tend to interpret events in the most negative way, see the future as bleak and unchangeable and be very harsh and critical about yourself. So understandably your mood gets dragged down even more. These ideas about negative thinking are central to the ideas of cognitive behavioural therapy, a form of psychological treatment that has been shown to be very helpful for depression. The strategies described in this book have their basis in this kind of treatment.

Emotions

Feelings such as sadness, despair and hopelessness are common. You may become anxious, feel emotionally 'flat' or feel as if you 'don't care'. You may often feel irritable and angry.

These emotions make negative thinking more likely and more severe, creating a vicious circle – negative thinking causes negative emotions, which in turn make negative thinking worse. This vicious circle is thought to be one of the most important factors in keeping depression going.

Combined with negative thoughts, emotions may also sap motivation and energy, so that it becomes harder and harder to do anything or to feel that anything is worthwhile or enjoyable. This can result in less social and general activity, less effort in taking care of yourself and thoughts like 'It's not even worth trying'.

Physical symptoms

Physical changes often accompany mood changes. Sleep problems are very common. When sleep quality is poor, you tend to lack energy and are easily exhausted by normal activities. In addition, it can seem very hard to deal with problems – even the everyday ones.

You may also experience a change in appetite. If you don't feel hungry and cut down on the amount of food you eat, you may experience an even greater loss of energy and become even less active. Or, if you comfort eat, you may gain weight, which might make you feel even worse.

Life situation

Difficult life situations sometimes cause depression and make it harder to solve problems. Nothing actually changes in terms of what's causing the stress, but once you're depressed these problems may seem insurmountable. Depression can also cause new problems – for example, in relationships and at work.

Depression involves all areas of your life: your behaviour, thoughts, emotions, physical well-being and life situation. These are all connected and, as a result, changes in one area lead to changes in another in a downward spiral. For example, losing your job might trigger low mood and a sense of discouragement, leading to negative thinking – 'The fact that I lost this job means I'm incompetent', 'No one will ever want to employ me again' or 'My family thinks I'm a failure and will probably leave me'. This inevitably leads to continuing, and perhaps worsening, depressive emotions, which leads to more negative thoughts and so on.

**Depressed   Negative
Mood   thoughts**

As this cycle continues, other changes may take place – worrying and brooding interferes with sleep, leading to fatigue and a lack of energy. You do less of the things you used to enjoy, taking away sources of pleasure and self-esteem. Even carrying out daily tasks seems like too much effort and, when you stop doing them, negative thoughts about being able to cope may emerge and even the smallest of tasks may seem too much. Hopelessness and misery grow.

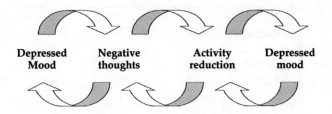

| Depressed Mood | Negative thoughts | Activity reduction | Depressed mood |

Negative changes in one area can cause the others to get worse as well. But the same cycle can work positively: when you are trying to get better, changes in one area can very often lead to improvement in the others. We could call this process the 'upward spiral'.

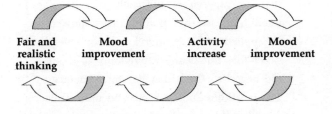

| Fair and realistic thinking | Mood improvement | Activity increase | Mood improvement |

The following are examples of people who have struggled with depression.

Patrick's story

Patrick was forty years old when he was first diagnosed with depression. Previously, he'd led a happy, productive life. He was married and enjoyed his work as an engineer; he enjoyed cycling and walking at weekends. His problems started when he was made redundant. Although the company had been having financial problems for some time, he was very surprised when he realised his position was being axed and began to worry that his performance had been below standard or that his supervisors and colleagues hadn't liked him. In the months that followed, he applied and was interviewed for several other jobs but wasn't offered any of them. He began to think that he was inadequate and worthless and, as more and more time passed without finding work, he began to feel hopeless. His feelings turned to despair when his wife was promoted in her job – instead of feeling pleased for her, he was just more convinced that he was useless. He avoided having conversations with his wife because he felt embarrassed by his unemployment. He stopped exercising and socialising and felt tired and listless most of the time. He stopped shaving and brushing his hair and then avoided going out at all because he thought he looked shabby. He eventually stopped applying for jobs because he thought it was 'pointless' – he believed that no one would want to hire him.

Kathy's story

Kathy was brought up in a large family. There wasn't a lot of money, so her mother had to go out to work on top of managing five children. Kathy often thought that her mother had no time for her, and began to believe that her mother did not love her as much as the others. She tried very hard to be good and to please her mother. Kathy became depressed for the first time shortly after the birth of her second child. Her depression was treated with medication, which was some help. Her husband was supportive and she enjoyed spending time with her two little daughters and this seemed to help keep the depression at bay. When the children were older, Kathy returned to work as a nurse, which she enjoyed at first, but after a while things started to go wrong. The charge nurse on her ward was very demanding and quite critical, which Kathy found quite stressful. She began to think that she was being 'picked on' and 'couldn't do anything right'. She worried that the charge nurse thought the other nurses were better than her, and liked them more. She began to feel more and more down and eventually she had to stop working. She was overwhelmed by thoughts that no one liked her or cared about her, and that she was 'useless'. The more she thought about these things, the worse she felt. She found that she was becoming very sensitive and often overreacted to comments made by her husband and daughters, which led to thoughts that she was a bad wife and mother and that her family found her irritating and a burden. She felt unmotivated most of the time and found it difficult to keep up with the housework. She stopped making the effort to spend time with her family and friends, and instead spent most of her time alone in her room.

5

Different Treatments for Depression

You may find that your depression goes away on its own without any treatment; however, some help can be very useful. Two of the most common treatments for depression are medication and psychological therapy.

Medication

Medication can work well for many people. This may be partly because it reduces the depressive symptoms enough to enable you to sort out the problems in your life that are contributing to the depression – it gives a sort of 'chemical leg-up'. But medication is seldom a complete treatment; it's very important for you to make changes in your life as well. For many people, the most effective treatment is a combination of medication and psychological therapy.

Psychological therapy

Many depressions can be treated without medication. Increasing activity, challenging negative thinking and dealing with problems directly all help lift depression.

There are many different psychological treatments available for depression. This book is based on cognitive behavioural treatment (CBT), a widely used form of therapy that focuses on thinking and behaviour, which often play a very important role in the onset and maintenance of depression. There is also strong evidence from research that CBT is an effective treatment for depression.

This book will help you work on improving your thoughts, behaviour and mood, either on your own or with the help of a mental health professional or your doctor. If you've got a friend or relative who's willing to help you, give them a copy and discuss your progress and any problems with them as you try out the different strategies.

It's helpful to write things down, and Part 2 of the book contains several exercises, with worked examples to guide you. Keep a notebook handy so you can keep a record of your thoughts, feelings and progress as suggested in the exercises.

Part 2: COPING WITH DEPRESSION

6

Reactivating Your Life

A reduction in activity tends to lead to an increase in depressive symptoms and inactivity tends to make symptoms worse. It's a vicious circle:

Depressed   Inactivity

So – don't wait until you feel better or have more energy to start doing more! Try increasing your activity gradually now, even though you may not feel like it. Sometimes, the less you feel like doing something, the more important it is to do it.

Think about what has changed in your life since you started feeling depressed. There may be many things that you are doing less and perhaps some things that you have stopped doing altogether. Have you:

- seen family and friends less than you used to?

- stopped doing any hobbies you enjoy?

- stopped taking care of yourself? For example, are you exercising and eating properly? Are you making an effort to look good?

- put the 'small things' on hold because they seem overwhelming?

These are just a few of the activities that typically tend to fall by the wayside when people start to feel low and unmotivated. You may be able to think of others.

So what do you do? This chapter covers three possible strategies: goal-setting, keeping track of your activities and gradually increasing physical activity.

Goal-setting

This goal-setting exercise will help you plan a gradual return to activity.

Step 1

Start by making a list in your notebook of things in your life that have slowed down or stopped since you started feeling depressed. For example, you may have stopped returning phone calls, wearing make-up or shaving regularly; perhaps you used to enjoy going to see films and haven't gone to the cinema in weeks. Now choose three activities from your list that you'd like to start working on, picking the activities that will be the easiest for you to start doing right away. Write these down.

Step 2

Having picked three activities, it's important to set specific and manageable goals. When you're depressed, you will have less energy and lower motivation than usual. It's very likely that it will feel difficult to get moving again. So set lower goals than you would if you weren't depressed.

For example, you may have written something like 'I've stopped doing the housework and want to set a goal to get the house cleaned up'. This will probably seem a very daunting task and difficult to achieve. Remember, your energy levels are low and you may not feel very motivated. So, a specific and manageable first goal might be to vacuum one room, or clear the paper off one table. That's it. The trick is to start with small steps and build up gradually.

Remember Patrick? Here's his list of neglected activities and the goals he set:

Activities I do less often or have stopped completely	Goal
Shaving and brushing hair	Shave and brush hair every morning
Returning emails	Send one email tomorrow afternoon
Dealing with the post and bills	On Wednesday morning, spend thirty minutes opening the post and sorting out which bills need to be paid

---

Tip

It's a good idea to decide in advance when you will carry out your goal, as well as how often or for how long you will do the activity.

Write down some goals for the coming week, keeping them specific and manageable.

_____

_____

_____

_____

_____

_____

_____

Step 3

Now it's time to carry out your goals. Check off each one as you complete it. Congratulate yourself. You've done something you wouldn't have done last week, and it probably wasn't easy.

Tip

Run into difficulty achieving your goal? Perhaps you set it too high in terms of your mood or energy levels or maybe it was a bit too vague. Ask yourself what went wrong. Then rework your goal, scaling it down if necessary. Remember, the most important thing is to start moving, no matter how slowly. As you start to feel better, you can start setting more challenging goals.

Step 4

After working on your goals, think about goals for the next week.

Ask yourself:

- Do I want to make my goals a little bit more challenging?

- Do I want to keep my goals at the same level for now? A good idea if you think it's important to feel a bit more confident and comfortable before moving on.

- Do I want to scale back my goals if I had trouble with them last week?

- Am I ready to add one or two new goals? If you decide to add a new goal or two, remember to make them specific and manageable.

Write out your goals for the next week and check off each one as you complete it. Remember to congratulate yourself each time you complete a goal. At the end of the week, repeat the process again. Try to set three goals for each week (some of these can be reworked or repeated goals from the previous weeks).

_____

_____

_____

_____

_____

_____

_____

Keeping track of your activities

When you're depressed you may have trouble believing you're accomplishing anything at all. Start rating what you're doing, what you're enjoying and what you're accomplishing. One way to do this is to record exactly what you do, hour by hour. Try this for a few days. Each time you write something down, give it two ratings out of ten – one for **enjoyment (E)**, and the other for **achievement (A)**. A 0 rating for enjoyment means you didn't enjoy the activity at all and 10 means the activity was extremely enjoyable. A 0 rating for achievement means you didn't feel you had achieved anything at all, while 10 means you successfully accomplished the task.

A couple of tips:

- Record the ratings at the time of the event. If you wait until later, your depression may cause you to discount or forget what you've done or how you felt (remember that depression affects how you think about things).

- Things seem more difficult when you are depressed – so a task you once found easy may now seem quite a challenge. If you manage to accomplish such a task, you should give yourself credit!

Your record of activities gives you information on what you are actually doing and enjoying. You may find that you're more active and competent or you're doing more things that you enjoy than you thought. Or you might find that you're doing very little and not enjoying yourself at all. In either case, this is a good time to set some goals, trying to do a little bit more and planning activities for specific times during the day.

In our example, Kathy was sure that she wasn't doing much during the day, which added to her belief that she was 'useless'. Here's her diary for the first two days:

Kathy's activity diary, with achievement (A) and enjoyment (E) ratings		
	Monday Achievement (A)/ Enjoyment(E)	**Tuesday** Achievement (A)/ Enjoyment (E)
8–9 a.m.	Got up, showered A3 E2	
9–10 a.m.	Washed up, put washing on A3 E3	Got up, showered A3 E2

10–11 a.m.	Went to shops A5 E2, drove to Mum's A5 E2	Cleaned bathroom A7 E2
11–12 noon	Talked to Mum and sister A5 E5	Hoovered the lounge A7 E2
12–1 p.m.	Took Mum to lunch for her birthday A5 E7	Had lunch A2 E4
1–2 p.m.		
2–3 p.m.	Gave Mum a computer lesson A7 E6	Had a rest and read A0 E6
3–4 p.m.		Did ironing A3 E3
4–5 p.m.	Drove home, cooked tea A3, E3	Prepared and cooked tea A5, E3
5–6 p.m.	Watched TV A0 E3	Watched TV A0 E2
6–7 p.m.	Watched TV A0 E3	Watched TV A0 E4
7–8 p.m.	Watched TV A0 E6	Watched TV A0 E5

Kathy was surprised to see that she was actually doing quite a lot and sometimes even getting a sense of achievement from what she was doing. She was able to use this information to tackle the suggestion that she was useless. Her diary also helped her realise that she was spending very little time with her husband and daughters, so she decided to set a goal to arrange some 'family time' during the evenings.

If, when you fill in your diary, you realise that you aren't doing very much, add small activities to your daily routine that give you higher levels of enjoyment and achievement. Here are a few other tips:

- Are you a morning person or an afternoon person? When is your energy level at its highest? Plan your activities accordingly.

- If your activity plan is very busy don't forget to schedule in some time for rest. We all need some time to unwind!

Increasing your physical activity

Exercise can help you recover from depression. Sometimes the improvement in mood happens quickly; sometimes it takes a few weeks. Exercise raises your energy level, improves physical well-being and provides a sense of accomplishment.

Regular exercise in the long term can help prevent depression from happening again.

Consider the pointers below when planning an exercise routine:

- Talk to your doctor before you start.

- Choose activities you enjoy: you'll be much more likely to stick with them. You may like to choose several different activities and switch between them to prevent things from getting boring.

- It's easier to stick with an exercise plan if your activities don't require a lot of preparation. For example, don't pick swimming if the nearest pool is twenty-five miles away – if you already own a pair of shoes suitable for walking, then going for a twenty-minute walk would be a lot easier to organise.

- Regular short periods of exercise (three to four times a week) are better than infrequent longer periods.

Patrick used to exercise regularly before his problems with depression but since losing his job he had virtually stopped all physical activity. Because he enjoyed cycling and walking, he decided that he should start by gradually picking up these activities again. His exercise plan looked like this:

Patrick's exercise plan		
Week 1	Monday	Go for a ten-minute bike ride
	Wednesday	Go for a fifteen-minute walk
	Saturday	Go for a fifteen-minute walk with my wife
Week 2	Monday	Go for a fifteen-minute bike ride
	Wednesday	Go for a twenty-minute bike ride (evening)
	Sunday	Go for a thirty-minute bike ride
Week 3	Monday	Go for a thirty-minute bike ride
	Wednesday	Go for a thirty-minute walk
	Friday	Go for a thirty-minute bike ride
	Sunday	Go for a one-hour walk with my wife

Patrick found that making a specific exercise plan made it more likely that he would stick to his goal of increasing his physical activity. It was difficult to motivate himself to 'get out there' the first few times, but it got easier the more he did it. After a month of regular exercise, he noticed that he felt a sense of achievement. He was also sleeping better and felt less exhausted.

In your notebook write down an exercise plan for the next few weeks. Use your goal-setting skills (see pages 28–33). Remember: exercise won't change your mood overnight. Take it slowly and gradually.

7

Negative Thinking and Depression

Each of us is affected differently by events, depending on how we think about them. For example, imagine that Mary is walking down the street and sees a friend – but the friend walks by without acknowledging her. Mary thinks to herself, 'Oh, dear, she must be angry with me. Or perhaps she doesn't like me and is trying to avoid me. I've lost another friend. I will always be alone.' Mary feels awful – she notices her sadness and loneliness growing. Now, imagine that Sarah encounters the same situation. Sarah thinks to herself, 'Wow – she's really distracted! I bet she's still thinking about that date she had last week.' Sarah feels a bit amused and goes about her day.

Note that the event that Mary and Sarah experienced was *the same event*; but their feelings about it were very different. This is because they *interpreted* it differently.

When you're depressed, you think very negatively. This thinking is very often *unfair* – for example, positive events are ignored and negative events emphasised – and *unrealistic* – for example, thinking is based on guesswork and exaggeration and even small problems are blown out of proportion.

Depression is associated with biased ways of interpreting events and situations. For example, when you're depressed you:

- think about yourself in a very critical fashion and judge yourself in a harsh and unfair manner. The negative things you've done are very obvious, but you've difficulty seeing anything positive about yourself.

- see the world around you in an unrealistically pessimistic way, emphasising its negative aspects and ignoring more promising aspects.

- anticipate a future that is bleak and disappointing.

Together, these ways of thinking are called 'the negative cognitive triad': thinking in an unfair and unrealistic way about yourself, your current situation and your future. These thoughts are biased and distorted.

Common forms of biased or distorted thinking include:

- *Filtering.* Seeing only the bad and ignoring the good. You may single out the negative and ignore any good things you've done. You may see only your weaknesses and mistakes and disregard your strengths and accomplishments.

- *Over-generalisation.* One negative event indicates the beginning of an endless negative spiral. If you make a mistake, the whole project is a failure. If you have difficulty with one friend, nobody likes you.

- *All-or-nothing thinking.* You see things as black-and-white. There's no middle ground.

- *Blowing things out of proportion.* In your mind, every small problem becomes a major disaster. After making one wrong comment at a meeting, you think everyone thinks you're stupid and that you may lose your job.

- *Labelling.* Talking to yourself in a critical way, calling yourself names like 'stupid' or 'a failure'. You feel these labels sum you up.

- *Mind-reading.* You make the mistake of believing you know what others are thinking: it's about you and it's negative. You end up reacting to what you *imagine* they're thinking, without finding out their true reaction.

- *Fortune-telling.* You think you know what the future holds and it's not good. This can lead to feelings of hopelessness.

- *Disqualifying the positive.* Anything positive about you, or anything positive that happens, is countered by a negative comment. For example: 'I did manage to get some things done – but anyone could have done that.'

- *Personalisation.* If something bad happens, it must have been your fault. Other, more likely causes are ignored.

- *Shoulds and oughts.* You spend a lot of time thinking about how you *should* be and how the world *ought to* be – but you are not and neither is the world. 'I should not upset people'. 'I ought to have achieved more than this'. This kind of thinking can be very discouraging.

Have a look through the list and see if you can identify some mistakes that you make.

This isn't a complete list – you may use kinds of distorted thinking that aren't described here.

Biased and distorted thoughts can happen so quickly that they seem to appear out of nowhere and are sometimes called *negative automatic thoughts*. Automatic thoughts aren't the result of reasoning or decision-making and sometimes they are so automatic they are difficult to identify. Unfortunately, at first glance these thoughts can also seem very plausible, which can make it tempting to believe them.

A three-step plan to overcome negative thinking

Step 1: Recognise your negative thoughts and how they trigger depressed mood

Because negative thinking is often automatic, you may not always realise that you're doing it. It's important to become aware of negative thinking patterns and how they are affecting your mood. A good way to help to identify negative thinking is to fill out a 'thought record' like the one on page 47 over the course of a week. Every time you notice your mood getting worse write down:

- the date

- the situation you are in

- what was going through your mind just then?

- the emotions you're feeling. Rate each one on a scale from 0 to 100 so that you'll be able to remember how strongly you felt that way.

Try to complete your thought record as soon as you can. If you wait, it'll be harder to remember exactly what you were thinking.

Keep this record for a week. At the end of the week look at your negative thoughts. Do you notice similar kinds of thoughts repeating themselves? Using the list of kinds of distorted thinking (pages 42–4), try to pinpoint any mistakes you made in your thinking. Watch for the same kind of mistake happening over and over again. This will help you identify the most common kinds of negative thinking that you use.

Identifying automatic thoughts

Sometimes it's difficult to identify automatic thoughts. Here are some questions you can ask yourself to help you figure out what your automatic thoughts are:

- What was going through my mind right before I started to feel this way?

- What does this say about me?

- What does this mean about my life? About my future?

- What I am afraid might happen?

- What is the worst thing that could happen if this is true?

- What does this mean about what the other person thinks or feels about me?

- What does this mean about other people in general?

Below is an example of one of Kathy's thought records.

Date	Situation What was going through my mind just then? Record thought, and if you like, try to classify the kind of distortion	Negative thought	Emotion Rate how strongly you feel that emotion (1–100 scale)
1st Oct.	Due to meet sister for lunch, but she's very late.	She forgot about me. (Mind-reading)	Sad – 100%
		She doesn't like me. (Mind-reading)	Lonely – 90%
		No one likes me. (Over-general-isation) I'm not important. (Labelling)	Hopeless – 90%

Step 2: Challenge your negative thoughts and learn to think in a more fair and realistic way

Challenging negative thinking patterns means you have to examine the situation from an objective viewpoint. You'll need to notice the mistakes you've made in your thinking and take steps to correct them. You'll also learn to examine the evidence for your negative thoughts and decide whether these are fair and realistic. You'll then try to come up with a more fair and realistic thought – based on the evidence, not on distorted thinking.

Challenging negative thoughts and replacing them with more fair and realistic ones isn't easy – it takes practice but the more you do it the easier it gets.

Thought-challenging is easiest if you use a step-by-step process. Kathy's thought record on the next page shows you how to do this. Copy the headings into your notebook, then note the date and the situation. Next, write down the negative thoughts that seem to be related to how you feel (you can categorise the type of distortion if you want). Then record your emotion and rate its intensity.

The next step is the most important: *Think about the situation and try to come up with a more fair and realistic alternative*. Sometimes this is as simple as reminding yourself that you don't have enough information to

	Example of a thought record to challenge negative thinking (Kathy)			
Date	Situation	Negative thought	Emotion	Fair and realistic thought	Emotion (rate 1–100)
1st Oct.	Due to meet sister for lunch, but she's very late.	She forgot about me. (Mind-reading)	Sad – 100%	I don't know why she's late: maybe something urgent came up.	Sad – 40%
		She doesn't like me. (Mind-reading)	Lonely – 90%	She has done lots of things to show that she really does care about me. For example, she phoned me a few days ago to suggest lunch.	Lonely – 20%
		No one likes me. (Over-generalisation)	Hopeless – 90%	It's only lunch, not the end of the world.	Hopeless – 40%
		I'm not important. (Labelling)		Some people do seem to like me. Just because she's late for lunch doesn't mean I'm not important. I am important: I'm a wife and a mother and I do have friends.	

be sure you know what is happening! This process is similar to having an argument with yourself – fight your negative thinking by giving yourself a chance to think fairly and realistically about what has happened. Finally, re-assess how you feel after coming up with some alternative, more rational, ways of thinking. Use a thought-challenging record to do this, like the one used by Kathy below.

Here are some questions you can ask yourself to make it easier to come up with more fair and realistic thoughts:

Testing the reality of negative automatic thoughts

- What evidence do you have for this thought? What about evidence that does not support this thought? Based on this evidence, what would be a fairer and more realistic thought?

- What would other people say about your negative thought? Would they say that the evidence supports this thought? If not, what would they say?

- Is there any other way of looking at this? Maybe there are several possibilities. What are they?

- Is there an alternative explanation? What is it?

- What is a less extreme way of looking at this situation? (Watch out for extreme and rarely true thoughts like 'I never do anything right'.) Try to be as realistic as possible.

- How would somebody else react to this situation? Ask around and find out.

- What would you tell somebody else if they were worried about this?

- Are you setting yourself an unrealistic standard? What would be more reasonable?

- Are you forgetting relevant facts? Are you focusing too strongly on irrelevant facts? Try to consider all the relevant information and put aside issues that aren't important.

- Are you thinking in all-or-nothing terms?

- Are you overestimating your responsibility in this situation? What is a more realistic assessment of your responsibility?

- What if this happens? What would be so bad about that?

- How will things be in X months'/years' time?

- Are you overestimating how likely this event is?

- Are you underestimating how well you can deal with this problem/situation?

- What are the results of thinking this way? If you think about it another way, would you have better results?

You've probably been thinking negatively for some time now, so that you don't even notice you are doing it. Challenging negative thoughts and coming up with more fair and realistic thoughts will help you feel better, but it's going to take practice. You may start to notice a difference in how you feel after a few weeks. This can be very encouraging, but it's very important to *keep practising*. If you stop, you may forget some of what you learned and have to start all over again.

Overcoming unrealistic negative thinking does *not* mean replacing it with unrealistic positive thinking – 'Everybody loves me', 'Nothing bad will ever happen'! Like negative thinking, unrealistic positive thinking is an inappropriate reaction to life. The aim is to judge yourself and your life in a realistic manner.

What if your negative thoughts are realistic?

Although much depressed thinking tends to follow a distorted pattern, it does not mean that negative or unpleasant thoughts are *always* wrong or unrealistic – just mostly! You may find it helpful to rate your thought on a scale of 1 to 10 for its basis in reality. For instance, imagine that, while walking down the street, you see Pete on the other side of the road and he doesn't respond to your 'Hello!' Because you're depressed, you may immediately think that Pete didn't say 'hello' back because he doesn't like you. But there may be other possible reasons – for example, he didn't hear you, he was daydreaming or he was in a mad rush. Which possible reason is the most fair and realistic?

Your 1 to 10 'reality' scale should go something like this. A score of 1 to 3 means that there is little or no

real evidence for Pete disliking you. If so start consid-
ering other, less harsh, explanations for his behaviour.

A score between 4 and 6 means that it's based at
least on some reality, but is probably biased by
distorted thinking. It's still important to examine
your initial negative thought and evaluate the evidence. A more fair and realistic thought might be:
'Pete has always been a good friend so it's highly
likely that he may not have heard me, but there
is an equal chance that he may be also be upset
because I haven't returned any of his phone calls
for two weeks because I have been feeling so down,
so maybe I need to check it out.' Then consider
problem-solving – ring Pete and find out what he's
really thinking. If he's upset that you haven't called,
maybe you can arrange to meet for coffee.

If you judge your thought at between 7 and 10,
it means that there's a lot of realistic evidence that
Pete doesn't like you (for instance, the last time you
met he may have told you that he didn't want to
see you again under any circumstances). This rec-
ollection may be very unpleasant and upsetting for
you, but it shows that your thoughts about Pete
are not part of a distorted thinking pattern. What
next? At this point, it's important to minimise the
risk of continuing from a realistic – but painful –
thought to more negative and distorted thoughts.

For example, you would want to avoid *overgeneralising* – just because Pete doesn't like you does not mean that everyone feels that way.

Step 3: Prepare for 'trigger' situations

There are some other ways you can improve your effectiveness at thought-challenging.

Plan in advance

If you can predict that an event or situation is likely to trigger negative thinking, you can prepare for it. Think about the negative thoughts you are likely to have and then work on coming up with more fair and realistic thoughts. Review your notes and practise the 'rational' thoughts prior to the event or situation.

Watch for 'typical' triggers

Review your past thought records and look for patterns. Do certain kinds of situation seem to set you off? If so, make a note of these 'typical' triggers. When you find yourself in such situations, deliberately rehearse your fair and realistic thoughts. This is a good way to weaken even very strong negative thinking patterns.

Tip

How to think fairly and realistically

At first, it may be hard to remember your fair and realistic thinking when you are in the midst of negative thinking. One thing you can try is writing down your fair and realistic thoughts on a cue-card that you can carry with you. When you catch yourself thinking negatively, pull out your card (you can always sneak away to the loo so that you can have some privacy) and remind yourself what kinds of thoughts are fair and realistic. Another strategy is to carry a list of questions to ask yourself about your thinking (see page 46). These kinds of things can help you get started. After you get the hang of it, you can leave the cue-cards at home.

8

Problem-solving

When you get depressed, your ability to solve problems becomes less effective. Sometimes this means you can't deal with the problems that started the depression in the first place, but often it expands to difficulty in dealing with many problems common in daily life.

There are many reasons why this happens. When you're depressed, you may feel tired and lack energy and have problems with concentration, memory and decision-making. Loss of confidence and low motivation are also major barriers to problem-solving.

Dealing with problems in your life makes you feel more effective, hopeful and encouraged. But it's very important to remember that your problem-solving resources are depleted at the moment. Tackling the problems in your life can be made more manageable by following the steps outlined below.

Step 1: What are the problems?

The first step is to figure out exactly what the problems are. Make a list. Include both the big and the small problems, even if they seem trivial or embarrassing. Don't spend time thinking about them – just list each one and move on. You don't have to come up with the solutions yet – just note the problems!

Patrick came up with all sorts of problems. Here are a few of them:

1. I'm unemployed

2. The garage door is broken

3. The printer is broken

4. The bills are overdue

5. I need a haircut

Step 2: Choose a problem to work on

Now select a problem from the list. Choose one that you could start working on right away. Don't worry about all the others; you can move on to those later on.

Write down the problem you've selected.

Now review your personal resources. Have you solved similar problems in the past? How? Did you have any personal strengths that made it easier? Are there any people who might be able to help or support you in this (these people wouldn't solve the problem for you, but rather help you solve the problem yourself)? Who?

Write down any possible resources you can use to solve your problem.

_____

_____

_____

_____

_____

_____

_____

_____

Now think about things that you could do that might help this situation. Write down as many possible ideas as you can – don't worry if they seem unlikely to work or aren't likely to solve the problem completely. Write them all down!

_____

_____

_____

_____

_____

_____

_____

_____

Patrick decided to work on one of his biggest problems – his unemployment. He considered his resources, including his experience with looking for work in the past, the skills and work experience he already possessed, and his old work colleagues who might be able to help. He came up with several possible solutions:

1. Look for a job similar to my last.

2. Look for a job that's in a different area but uses my computer skills.

3. Look for part-time jobs as well as full-time jobs.

4. Look into further education – maybe it would be easier to find a job if I developed some new skills.

Step 3: Choose a solution

Next, you need to choose one of your possible solutions. Think about the pros and cons to each and consider whether you have the energy and resources needed to carry them out. You don't have to solve the problem completely right now, only move in the right direction.

Write down your choice.

_____

_____

_____

_____

_____

_____

_____

_____

Patrick decided to look for a job similar to his last position. He chose this solution because he had lots of experience and skills that he thought would increase his chances of being hired and he had ex-work colleagues he could ask about possible job openings.

Step 4: Make a detailed plan of action

It's useful to break down the plan into specific and manageable steps. Then you can start at the beginning and work through each step, one at a time. This makes the task seem less overwhelming and helps you get started.

Patrick began by breaking down his plan into the following steps:

1. Go to the local shop and buy a newspaper this afternoon.

2. Tonight, have a look at the adverts and see what's available.

3. Tomorrow, have a look at job adverts on the internet.

4. Tomorrow evening, call Sam (ex-work colleague) to ask if he knows of any job openings.

5. Decide which jobs to apply for by the end of the week.

6. Spend one hour updating my CV on Tuesday.

7. Ask my wife to have a look at my CV and make suggestions.

In your notebook, break down your plan into specific and manageable steps, numbering them separately to keep them distinct in your mind. *Remember: You don't have to solve the problem completely right now; your plan need only move you in the right direction.*

_____

_____

_____

_____

_____

_____

_____

_____

Step 5: Putting the plan into action

Remember to keep your goals manageable and begin carrying out the plan over the coming week.

Evaluate every step as you go – what happened? What was the outcome? Is it time to move to the second step, or should you adapt your plan? Even if a step doesn't work as well as you hoped, you've probably learned something that will help you make a better plan next time.

Tip

Watch out for negative thoughts!

Remember, when you're depressed, negative thoughts are likely to pop into your mind. Write them down. Then evaluate them – use the skills you worked on in the last section. How is this thinking holding you back? Try to evaluate the problem *and* your ability to solve it in a fair and realistic way.

After a week has passed, work out how things are going.

- Did your plan work? If so, it's time to move to the next step. Or, if the problem is solved, go back to your problem list and start again with a new problem.

- Did you run into problems? If so, maybe you need to revise your goal and try again. If it was too difficult, make it a bit easier.

- Maybe you just need to try the same plan again. Is there a reason why it would be more likely to work this week?

- Maybe you need to take a whole new approach. If you think this is the case, try going back to Step 2.

After you have evaluated how things went last week, it is time to decide on the next step. Write it down.

Keep working on the problem in this way. Keep the steps to solving the problem specific and manageable. Remember to tackle the steps one at a time – this will help prevent you feeling overwhelmed. Congratulate yourself for any progress you make!

When you decide it is time to start working on a new problem, look back at your problem list. Select something to work on, and follow the steps of problem-solving.

9

Recognising the Positive

Keeping track of good things that happen

One of the very unfair things about depression is that your brain deals with positive information and negative information very differently. If someone criticises you, you're likely to accept it as true. But if someone says something nice to you, you manage to discount the positive comment completely. And then, without meaning to, you are quite likely to forget it happened at all. So – all you notice and remember are the negative things and the general picture that gets built up is therefore overwhelmingly negative.

To combat this, you need to start keeping track of the good things that happen in your life. It can also be helpful to remind yourself about the things that are generally positive in your life, and the things that you are grateful for, but perhaps take for granted. This will allow you to develop a **fairer, realistic and positive** view of yourself and your situation. Keep a daily list – try to write down at least three things. This will be very hard! At first, you may think that the things you write down are silly or trivial or don't mean anything. But it's important to write them down anyway! Over time, you may realise that there are more positive occasions than you once noticed – and many that you previously ignored.

You'll want to record times when:

- you manage to get something done

- something you do goes according to plan

- something you do goes better than expected

- you do something that's worthwhile

- somebody contacts you

- somebody compliments you.

You will also want to remind yourself about good things in your life or things you are grateful for, such as:

- people in your life who you love

- people in your life who care about you

- other things about your situation that are positive and you are grateful for, which might include your job, your home, your physical health or the physical health of your family and friends or your upcoming holiday.

Remember, nothing is too small or too trivial to go on this list! Recognising and appreciating the positive is important, no matter how insignificant it might seem. It is important to do this every day.

Reward yourself!

Finding a way to give yourself positive rewards is important. Tackling depression is hard work and you deserve to reward yourself for any accomplishments you make or for any positive changes you notice in yourself – such as changes in your thinking, behaviour or mood. When you are treated well, you feel better. This is true even if the person treating you well is yourself. You give yourself the message that you're worth it and that's very important.

Of course, your ability to give yourself positive rewards may be limited by lack of money or time or other practical problems but there may be some things you can do. What about going for a walk when the sun is shining? Or having a nice bath? Or spending half an hour reading a book? Think about what you might enjoy – then do it!

Keep a record of any successes and positive changes you make (including *efforts* to change) and the rewards you give yourself. Watch out for thoughts like, 'I don't deserve a reward for this – this is something I should be doing anyway'. Remember, things are more difficult when you are depressed and any effort to modify your thoughts or behaviour is hard work. Watch out as well for depressed – and depressing – thoughts like, 'I don't deserve anything nice; I shouldn't waste time or money on myself '.

Creating a more positive view of yourself

When you're depressed, it's very unusual to be able to name many good qualities about yourself. Most people can only come up with very negative qualities. In fact, it's not easy even when not depressed; many of us have grown up in a culture that frowns on people who 'blow their own trumpet' and encourages people to be modest about their achievements. This means that recognising your positive points can be doubly hard. If you were asked to think of ten good things about yourself you'd probably find it quite difficult. So it may be easier to start to build up a better image of yourself in another way. Try this exercise.

Look at the list of adjectives below and give yourself a rating for each. 0 means you have none of that quality, 1 means you have a little and 2 means you have quite a bit.

kind	not easily put off	artistic
assertive	forgiving	generous
flexible	clever	hard-working
helpful	intelligent	good manager
compassionate	well-read	honest
practical	mechanical	responsible
organised	sympathetic	genuine
quiet	cuddly	incisive
gentle	caring	thoughtful
forthright	entertaining	loving
attractive	funny	warm
tidy	creative	unselfish
efficient	giving	good listener
considerate	conscientious	imaginative
determined	loyal	good housekeeper
forceful	good cook	
		punctual

Now go through the list, and pick out all the qualities you rated with a 2 or a 1 and write them down.

_____

_____

_____

_____

_____

_____

There are, of course, many other good qualities about people that are not on this list. If some of your good qualities aren't included here, that doesn't mean that they're not important! If you think of any other positive personal qualities that aren't on the list, add them and give yourself a rating.

You may have made a number of ratings of 2 and 1 or perhaps only a few. But even if you only have one or two, then that's a start. These are good qualities about yourself that you can use to start building up a better, more positive picture of yourself.

How do your friends and family see you? How would they rate you on that list? Would they have more positive things to say about you? Sometimes it's helpful to think about what a good friend would say. If you feel brave enough, show the list to a friend or family member and ask them to rate you. Compare that list of ratings to your own.

Now try writing your good qualities out on a card. Look at it as often as you can. Instead of listening to the voice in your head that says you're useless and a failure or whatever insult it prefers, try to think of your positive qualities. If you can make yourself rehearse your good qualities as often as you do the bad ones, then you might come to believe there are some positive things about you.

_____

_____

_____

_____

_____

_____

_____

A Final Word of Encouragement

This booklet provides information about depression and introduces you to strategies that have been shown to be effective in tackling depression. These strategies focus primarily on changing the way you think and the way you act. They are not easy – in fact, it takes a lot of practice to master the skills discussed here. It's important to keep practising these strategies in order to make them easier and more automatic. It's also important to remind yourself of what you have learned once you are feeling better – carrying on using the skills will help prevent it happening again.

We hope that this book has been useful and wish you the very best of luck. No matter how hard it might be to believe it now, depression will get better!

Lee Brosan and Brenda Hogan

Other Things that Might Help

This booklet has provided you with an introduction to the problems caused by depression and what you can do to overcome them. Some people will find that this is all they need to do to see a big improvement, while others may feel that they need a bit more information and help, and in that case there are some longer and more detailed self-help books around. Ask your GP if there's a Books on Prescription scheme running in your area – if there isn't, we recommend the following books:

The Feeling Good Handbook by David D. Burns, published by Penguin

Overcoming Depression by Paul Gilbert, published by Robinson

The Complete CBT Guide for Depression and Low Mood edited by Lee Brosan and David Westbrook, published by Robinson

Mind Over Mood by Dennis Greenberger and Christine A. Padesky, published by Guilford Press

How to Stop Worrying by Frank Tallis, published by Sheldon Press

Sometimes the self-help approach works better if you have someone supporting you. Ask your GP if there's anyone at the surgery who would be able to work through your self-help book with you. Some surgeries have graduate mental health workers who would be able to help in this way, or who might offer general support. He or she is likely to be able to spend more time with you than your GP and may be able to offer follow-up appointments.

For some people a self-help approach may not be enough. If this is the case for you, don't despair – there are other kinds of help available.

Talk to your GP – make an appointment to talk through the different treatment options on offer to you. Your GP can refer you to an NHS therapist for cognitive behavioural therapy – most places now have CBT available on the NHS, although there can be a considerable waiting list. Don't be put off if you've not found working through a CBT-based self-help manual right for you – talking to a therapist can make a big difference. If an NHS therapist isn't available in your area or you'd prefer not to wait to see one, ask your GP to recommend a private therapist.

Although CBT is widely recommended for depression there are many other kinds of therapy available that you could also discuss with your GP.

Medication can be very helpful for some people and sometimes a combination of medication and psychological therapy can work wonders. However, you need to discuss this form of treatment and any possible side effects with your doctor to work out whether it's right for you.

The following organisations offer help and advice on depression and you may find them a useful source of information:

British Association for Behavioural and Cognitive Psychotherapies (BABCP)

Tel: 0161 705 4304

Email: babcp@babcp.com;

Website: www.babcp.com

Provides contact details for therapists in your area, both NHS and private.

Mind

Tel: 0300 123 3393

Website: www.mind.org.uk

Samaritans

Helpline: 116 123

Email: jo@samaritans.org

Website: www.samaritans.org.uk

Provides confidential, non-judgemental emotional support 24 hours a day by phone, text, email, letter or through a local branch (see website for details).

An Introduction to Coping with Anxiety

2nd Edition

Brenda Hogan and Lee Brosan

ISBN: 978-1-47214-024-1 (paperback)
ISBN: 978-1-47214-023-4 (ebook)

Anxiety is one of the most common mental health conditions worldwide, affecting millions of people each year. But it can be treated effectively with cognitive behavioural therapy (CBT). Written by experienced practitioners, this introductory book offers practical support for how to overcome your anxiety. It explains what anxiety is and how it makes you feel when it becomes unmanageable or lasts for long periods of time. It will also advise on how to spot and challenge thoughts that make you anxious, showing you how to change your behaviour in order to reduce your feelings of anxiety.

An Introduction to Coping with Insomnia and Sleep Problems

2nd Edition

Colin A. Espie

ISBN: 978-1-47213-854-5 (paperback)
ISBN: 978-1-47213-892-7 (ebook)

Poor sleep can have a huge impact on our health and well-being, leaving us feeling run-down, exhausted and stressed out. Written by a leading expert in the field, this simple guide explains the causes of insomnia and why it is so difficult to break bad habits. It gives you clinically proven cognitive behavioural therapy (CBT) techniques for improving the quality of your sleep, showing you how to keep a sleep diary, set personal goals, improve your sleep hygiene, deal with a racing mind and make lasting improvements to your sleeping and waking pattern.

An Introduction to Coping
with Panic

2nd Edition

Charles Young

ISBN: 978-1-47213-853-8 (paperback)
ISBN: 978-1-47213-954-2 (ebook)

Panic disorder and panic attacks affect huge numbers of people across the world. This self-help guide explains what panic attacks are, how they develop and what makes them persist. It uses clinically proven cognitive behavioural therapy (CBT) techniques to help you recognise the link between your thoughts and your periods of panic, enabling you to: spot and challenge these thoughts, keep a panic diary and learn calming breathing techniques.

An Introduction to Coping with Depression for Carers

Tony Frais

ISBN: 978-1-47211-933-9 (paperback)
ISBN: 978-1-47211-934-6 (ebook)

Looking after a person with depression can often leave carers emotionally and physically exhausted. This short, straightforward and easily understandable guide offers valuable advice on how carers can:

· better understand the nature of depression and how it affects both patient and carer

· have a clearer understanding of the treatment options for the patient, including medication and therapy

· lessen the impact of the illness on the carer's life

· find the help and support they need

· maintain their own well-being whilst supporting the patient through to recovery and beyond

Overcoming Depression

3rd Edition

Paul Gilbert

ISBN: 978-1-84901-066-5 (paperback)

ISBN: 978-1-84901-155-6 (ebook)

If you suffer from depression you are far from alone. Depression is very common, affecting over 300 million people around the world.

Written by Professor Paul Gilbert, internationally recognised for his work on depression, this highly acclaimed self-help book has been of benefit to thousands of people including sufferers, their friends and families, and those working in the medical profession.

This fully revised third edition has been extensively updated and rewritten to reflect over ten years of new research on understanding and treating depression, particularly the importance of developing compassionate ways of thinking, behaving and feeling. It includes:

· Helpful case studies
· Easy-to-follow, step-by-step suggestions and exercises to help you understand your depression and lift your mood

The Complete CBT Guide for Depression and Low Mood

Lee Brosan and David Westbrook

ISBN: 978-1-78033-880-4 (paperback)

ISBN: 978-1-78033-881-1 (ebook)

Depression and low mood affect a significant portion of the general public. Sadly, those with depression often experience other problems such as low self-esteem and relationship difficulties. But however depression is affecting you, cognitive behavioural therapy (CBT) can help. CBT is used widely in the NHS and has been found to be extremely effective at helping people overcome depression and low mood.

This practical self-help book provides essential information about the nature of depression and covers a range of topics including insomnia, rumination, bipolar disorder and postnatal depression. It also contains information on treatments such as mindfulness, behavioural activation and compassion-focused therapy.